Mrs BEETON'S
HOME COOKING
FIRST COURSE
DISHES

WARD LOCK LIMITED · LONDON

© Ward Lock Limited 1986

First published in Great Britain
in 1986 by Ward Lock Limited,
8 Clifford Street,
London W1X 1RB,
an Egmont Company.

Edited by Susan Dixon
Designed by Melissa Orrom
Text filmset in Caslon 540
by Cheney & Sons Limited
Printed and bound in Italy by
L.E.G.O.

**British Library Cataloguing in
Publication Data**

First course dishes.—
(Mrs. Beeton's home cooking)
  1. Cookery (Appetizers)
  I. Series
  641.8'12   TX740

ISBN 0-7063-6453-8

Notes

The recipes in this book have
been tested in metric weights
and measures. These have
been based on equivalents of
25g to 1 oz, 500g to 1 lb and
500 ml to 1 pint, with some
adjustments where necessary.

It is important to follow *either*
the metric *or* the imperial
measures. Do not use a
combination of measures.

FIRST-COURSE DISHES

Great care should be taken, that, between the first and second courses, no more time is allowed to elapse than is necessary, for fear that the company in the dining-room lose all relish for what has yet to come of the dinner.

Isabella Beeton 1861

On pages 2 and 3
From the top, clockwise
Cucumber Cassolettes (page 56), Stuffed Eggs (page 37) and
Melon with Parma Ham (page 14)

FRUIT DISHES

GRAPEFRUIT BASKETS

4 helpings

2 large firm grapefruit
1 × 5cm/2 inch segment ripe
   Charentais *or* Ogen melon
225g/8oz canned pineapple cubes

1 orange
4 maraschino cherries
white *or* brown sugar *or* 4 × 10ml
   spoons/4 dessertspoons
   medium-dry sherry

DECORATION

mint sprigs

Cut the grapefruit in half crossways, and remove the pips. Snip out the cores with scissors. Remove the flesh from the halved skins, and snip out the membranes in the skins. Keep the halved skins aside, and put the flesh in a basin. Cut the melon flesh into 2.5 cm/1 inch cubes, drain the pineapple, and prepare the orange like the grapefruit. Halve the cherries. Mix all the fruit with the grapefruit flesh in the basin. Sweeten slightly if desired, or add the sherry. Pile the fruit (with any juice or sherry) back into the grapefruit skins. Chill before serving. Serve decorated with mint sprigs.

Grapefruit Baskets

GRAPEFRUIT COCKTAIL

6 helpings

3 grapefruit
50g/2oz sugar
3 × 15ml spoons/3 tablespoons
   boiling water

2 × 15ml spoons/2 tablespoons
   medium-dry sherry

DECORATION

6 maraschino cherries

6 mint sprigs

Cut the grapefruit in half crossways and remove the pips. Snip out the cores with scissors. Remove the flesh from the halved skin, and put in a basin. Dissolve the sugar in the water, add the sherry and pour the mixture over the fruit. Cover and chill until ready to serve. Spoon into suitable glasses, and decorate with the cherries and sprigs of mint before serving.

SPICED GRAPEFRUIT

4 helpings

2 large grapefruit
25g/1oz softened butter
25–50g/1–2oz brown sugar

½–1 × 5ml spoon/½–1 teaspoon
ground mixed spice

DECORATION

4 glacé *or* maraschino cherries

Cut the grapefruit in half crossways, and remove the pips. Snip out the cores with scissors. Spread the butter over the grapefruit, and sprinkle with the sugar and spice. Put under a hot grill for 4 minutes, or in a fairly hot oven at 200°C/400°F/Gas 6, for 10 minutes.

Decorate with the cherries, and serve at once.

CHERRY.

AVOCADO PEARS WITH PRAWNS OR AVOCADO ROYALE

4 helpings

2 × 15ml spoons/2 tablespoons
  olive oil
2 × 15ml spoons/2 tablespoons
  distilled vinegar
a pinch each of salt and pepper
a little mixed French mustard (not
  Dijon)
2 large avocado pears

a pinch of sugar (optional)
½ clove of garlic (optional)
100g/4oz peeled prawns, fresh,
  frozen *or* canned
crisp lettuce leaves

GARNISH
lemon wedges

Blend the oil, vinegar, and seasonings together. Halve and stone the pears, and brush all over with a little of the dressing. Add the sugar and crush and add the garlic to the remaining dressing, if used. Toss the prawns in this; then spoon into the pear halves. Place on crisp lettuce leaves. Garnish with lemon wedges.

Note Frozen prawns should be squeezed gently before using to get rid of any excess moisture.

Avocado Pears with Prawns

Avocado Pears and Soured Cream

2 avocado pears
1 × 5ml spoon/1 teaspoon lemon
  juice
1 × 5ml spoon/1 teaspoon salt
2 × 5ml spoons/2 teaspoons caster
  sugar

1 × 2.5 ml spoon/½ teaspoon dry
  mustard
a pinch of paprika
150ml/¼ pint soured cream *or*
  smetana

Halve the pears lengthways and remove the stones. Scoop all the
flesh out of the skins, and mash it with the lemon juice and half the
salt. Replace the flesh in the shells. To make the dressing, mix all
the remaining ingredients together until smooth. Top the pears
with the dressing.

Avocado Pears Vinaigrette

2 large, firm, ripe avocado pears
2 × 15ml spoons/2 tablespoons
  lemon juice

vinaigrette sauce

Make sure the pear are firm but ripe, and are not discoloured. If
they show any signs of over-ripeness such as being soft or
blackened, use them for a cooked dish.

Halve the pears lengthways and remove the stones. Brush the
halved pears with lemon juice immediately to prevent
discoloration. Serve 1 half pear per person, cut side uppermost on a
small plate, with a special avocado spoon, stainless steel or silver
teaspoon or a grapefruit spoon. Serve the vinaigrette sauce
separately.

MELON

Melon makes a refreshing starter throughout the year. The varieties most often used are the Cantaloup, honeydew, Ogen, Charentais, and watermelon. Melon should always be served lightly chilled, but it should not be too cold or it loses its delicate flavour.

To serve a large Cantaloup or honeydew melon, cut it in half lengthways, then cut into segments and remove the seeds with a spoon. Serve 1 segment per person; a large melon should supply 8 segments.

Serve the melon with the flesh attached to the skin, or cut the flesh from the skin with a sharp knife but leave the skin underneath the melon segment. The melon flesh can then also be cut into small pieces which are easier to eat.

Smaller melons, such as Ogen and Charentais, should just be cut in half crossways, and the pips scooped out with a spoon. They serve 2 people as a rule, although they can be cut into quarters, to serve four.

Watermelon should be cut into suitably sized segments. Small spoons should be provided for removing the seeds, as well as knives and forks for cutting up the melon.

Ripe melons may not require any sugar, but sugar can be served separately, with chopped stem ginger or ground ginger, or with lemon or lime.

THE LEMON.

MARINATED MELON

———— *4 helpings* ————

2 Ogen *or* Charentais melons   4 × 15ml spoons/4 tablespoons
                                             maraschino liqueur *or* port

Cut the melons in half crossways and scoop out the seeds. Spoon 1
× 15ml spoon/1 tablespoon of maraschino liqueur or port into the
centre and chill for 1 hour before serving. Sugar can be served with
the melons as well, if desired.

MELON WITH PARMA HAM

This is an elaborate dish using paper-thin slices of Parma or other
smoked ham. For each person, serve 3 loosely rolled slices of ham
arranged in a line alternately with 7 × 2.5cm/1 inch sticks of firm, ripe,
green-fleshed melon.

Marinated Melon

PEAR, NUT, AND DATE SALAD

6 helpings

3 ripe dessert pears *or* 6 canned
  pear halves
1 × 15ml spoon/1 tablespoon
  lemon juice
1 small crisp lettuce
100g/4oz stoned dates

50g/2oz shelled walnuts
1 × 10ml spoon/1 dessertspoon
  chopped parsley
3 × 15ml spoons/3 tablespoons
  French dressing

If using fresh pears, peel and halve them, and remove the cores
with a small spoon. Sprinkle lightly with the lemon juice to
preserve the colour. If using canned pears, drain off the juice, and
dry thoroughly. Wash the lettuce and dry thoroughly. Reserve 6
outside leaves and shred the rest. Mix with the dates, walnuts, and
parsley. Add the dressing and toss lightly. Arrange a lettuce leaf on
each of 6 individual plates and place the pear in the centre, with
the cut side uppermost. Pile in the date mixture and chill lightly
for 1 hour before serving.

THE WALNUT.

PEARS WITH STILTON

4 helpings

2 hard cooking pears	salt
50–75g/2–3oz Stilton cheese	fat for greasing
juice of 1 lemon	pepper

Peel the pears, cut in half lengthways, and remove the core and any pips. Cut each half pear into 3 or 4 thin slices lengthways. Cut the cheese into thin slices. Trim the cheese slices to fit the pears. Put to one side together with the trimmings. Simmer the pear slices in water with the lemon juice and a little salt. Remove them when softened at the edges but still firm in the centre.

· Grease a flat flameproof dish. Lay the pear slices in a circle with the narrower ends to the centre. Lay the cheese slices on top, and sprinkle with any cheese trimmings. Season very lightly with pepper (no salt). Grill under moderate heat for 3-5 minutes or until the cheese begins to bubble and brown. Serve at once.

Overleaf
From the top, clockwise
*Stuffed Tomato Salad (page 32), Pear, Nut and Date Salad (page 16)*and
Russian Salad (page 20)

VEGETABLE DISHES

RUSSIAN SALAD

4 helpings

1 small cooked cauliflower
3 boiled potatoes
2 tomatoes
50g/2oz ham *or* tongue (optional)
3 gherkins
a few lettuce leaves
4 × 15ml spoons/4 tablespoons
   peas

2 × 15ml spoons/2 tablespoons
   diced cooked carrot
2 × 15ml spoons/2 tablespoons
   diced cooked turnip
50g/2oz peeled prawns *or* shrimps
   (optional)
salt and pepper
3 × 15ml spoons/3 tablespoons
   mayonnaise

GARNISH

1 small diced cooked beetroot
50g/2oz smoked salmon, cut into
   strips (optional)
4 olives

1 × 15ml spoon/1 tablespoon
   capers
4 anchovy fillets (optional)

Break the cauliflower into small sprigs. Peel and dice the potatoes. Skin, de-seed, and dice the tomatoes. Cut the ham or tongue into small strips, if used. Chop the gherkins and shred the lettuce leaves. Put the vegetables, meat, and fish, if used, in layers in a salad bowl, sprinkling each layer with salt, pepper, and mayonnaise. Garnish with the remaining ingredients.

HOT STUFFED ARTICHOKE BASES

— 4 helpings —

8 small cooked *or* canned artichoke
   bases

butter for greasing
round slices of fried bread *or* toast

STUFFING

200g/7oz cooked short-grain rice
4 × 15ml spoons/4 tablespoons
   grated Parmesan cheese
2 × 15ml spoons/2 tablespoons
   pine nut kernels

lemon juice
salt and pepper

Re-heat the artichoke bases by steaming for 6–8 minutes, or bake
in a shallow dish in a cool oven under buttered paper for 15–18
minutes.

Meanwhile, make the stuffing. Mix together the rice, cheese,
and pine nut kernels, a little lemon juice, and seasoning to taste,
then heat gently.

Pile 1–2 × 15ml spoons/1–2 tablespoons of the hot stuffing in
each artichoke base, and serve immediately on the fried bread or
toast.

ARTICHOKES.

ASPARAGUS WITH HOT LEMON SAUCE

4–8 helpings

50 heads asparagus
250ml/½ pint milk
1 small lettuce
1 small onion (75g/3oz approx)
1 bay leaf
1 sprig of thyme
salt

25g/1oz butter
25g/1oz flour
1 egg
pepper
1 × 5ml spoon/1 teaspoon lemon juice
8 slices toasted *or* fried bread

GARNISH

chopped parsley   cucumber strips

Prepare the asparagus heads and tie them into bundles. Put the milk into a deep saucepan or asparagus pan. Shred the lettuce finely and skin and chop the onion. Add to the pan with the bay leaf, thyme, and a little salt. Bring the milk to the boil and put in the asparagus. Simmer gently for about 15 minutes or until the asparagus is tender. Remove from the pan and trim off all the inedible parts of the stalks. Untie, and keep the asparagus warm. Strain the milk.

Melt the butter in a small clean saucepan, stir in the flour, and cook gently for 1 minute. Draw off the heat and gradually stir in the strained milk. Return to the heat and stir all the time until the sauce thickens. Cool slightly, beat the egg until liquid, and stir it into the sauce. Season to taste, and add the lemon juice. Arrange the slices of toasted or fried bread on a warmed serving dish, and pile the asparagus on them. Coat with the sauce and garnish with chopped parsley and cucumber strips.

Asparagus with Hot Lemon Sauce

VEGETABLES À LA GRECQUE

500g/1lb vegetables (see **Note**)
½ × 2.5ml spoon/¼ teaspoon
  coriander seeds
1 clove of garlic
400g/13oz tomatoes
4 × 15ml spoons/4 tablespoons
  olive oil

2 × 15ml spoons/2 tablespoons
  lemon juice
150ml/6 fl oz water
1 bay leaf
1 sprig of thyme
salt and pepper

Prepare the vegetables. Slice courgettes, celery, fennel, and leeks; skin onions; leave button mushrooms whole or cut into halves or quarters; dice cucumber or aubergines.

Crush the coriander seeds, skin and crush the garlic, and skin and chop the tomatoes. Put the oil, lemon juice, water, bay leaf, thyme, coriander seeds, garlic, and seasoning into a saucepan. Bring to the boil. Add the tomatoes and cook, uncovered, over moderate heat for 25 minutes. If the vegetables are to be cooked and served hot, add for the appropriate time according to the type of vegetable. If they are already cooked and only need re-heating, or they are to be served raw but hot, add to the sauce for the final 2–3 minutes. If they are to be served cold, pour the hot sauce over the raw vegetables and leave to cool. Remove the bay leaf and thyme before serving.

Note Many different vegetables can be cooked *à la Grecque* and can be served hot or cold. Small portions are often served cold as a first course or as part of a mixed hors d'œuvre. The most usual ones are courgettes, celery, fennel, button onions and mushrooms, and red and green peppers. Cucumber, aubergines, and leeks are also popular.

CELERIAC IN MUSTARD DRESSING

4 helpings

1 medium-sized celeriac
3 × 2.5ml spoons/1½ teaspoons
  salt
3 × 2.5ml spoons/1½ teaspoons
  lemon juice
4 × 15ml spoons/4 tablespoons
  French mustard

3 × 15ml spoons/3 tablespoons
  boiling water
100ml/4 fl oz olive oil *or* as needed
2 × 15ml spoons/2 tablespoons
  white vinegar
salt and pepper

GARNISH

2 × 15ml spoons/2 tablespoons
  chopped mixed herbs *or* parsley

Peel the celeriac, and cut it into matchsticks. Toss the sticks in a bowl with the salt and lemon juice, and leave to stand for 30 minutes. Rinse in a strainer under cold running water, drain well, and pat dry. Put the mustard into a warmed bowl, and very gradually whisk in the boiling water. Then whisk in the oil drop by drop as when making mayonnaise, using enough to make a thick suace. Whisk in the vinegar in the same way. Season with salt and pepper. Fold in the celeriac matchsticks, cover loosely with a cloth, and leave in a cool place for several hours or overnight. Sprinkle the herbs over the dish before serving.

CUCUMBER IN SOURED CREAM

4 helpings

3 cucumbers
salt
1 × 5cm/2 inch piece fennel stem
  or 1 thick slice of the bulb
1 hard-boiled egg yolk

pepper
150ml/¼ pint soured cream
1 × 10ml spoon/1 dessertspoon
  cider vinegar *or* white wine
  vinegar

Slice the cucumbers very thinly, sprinkle with the salt; then leave for 30 minutes. Drain and pat dry. Slice the fennel thinly. Crumble the egg yolk coarsely and mix it with the fennel. Just before serving, sprinkle the cucumber with pepper, mix the soured cream with salt and the vinegar, and pour it over the cucumbers. Sprinkle with the fennel and egg.

Cucumber in Soured Cream

FELAFEL
(Deep-fried Chick-pea Balls)

FELAFEL

200g/7oz cooked chick-peas
75g/3oz fine matzo meal
1 × 5ml spoon/1 teaspoon salt
2 × 5ml spoons/2 teaspoons ground cumin

½ × 2.5ml spoon/¼ teaspoon ground coriander
½ × 2.5ml spoon/¼ teaspoon garlic powder
oil for deep frying

TAHINA SAUCE

50g/2oz ground sesame seeds
75ml/3 fl oz water
½ × 2.5ml spoon/¼ teaspoon garlic powder

½ × 2.5ml spoon/¼ teaspoon salt
1 × 15ml spoon/1 tablespoon lemon juice
a pinch of pepper

Mince the chick-peas finely or chop and sieve them. Add all the other ingredients for the felafel and form into small balls. Heat the oil to 170–175°C/338–347°F, and fry the felafel until golden-brown.

For the tahina sauce, mix all ingredients together, and sieve to make a smooth purée, or process in an electric blender for a few minutes. Re-season if required. Serve hot.

HUMMUS

6–8 helpings

300g/11oz cooked chick-peas
150ml/¼ pint tahina (sesame seed
   paste)
100ml/4 fl oz lemon juice
50ml/2 fl oz cooking liquid from
   chick-peas, if required

1 clove of garlic
salt
2 × 10ml spoons/2 dessertspoons
   olive oil
chopped parsley

Grind the chick-peas in a nut-mill, or crush in a pestle and mortar
to make a smooth paste. Alternatively, process the chick-peas in
an electric blender. In a mixing bowl, blend together the tahina
and lemon juice. The mixture should have the consistency of thick
cream. If it is too stiff, thin with some of the liquid from cooking
the chick-peas. Add the ground chick-peas. Skin and chop the
garlic and add to the chick-peas. Stir briskly until well blended.
Season with salt. Place the hummus in a shallow serving bowl,
trickle the olive oil over it, and sprinkle with chopped parsley.

   Serve with French bread, crispbread or pita bread.

GARLIC.

CRUDITÉS

These are small raw or blanched vegetables, cut up or grated, and served as a first course with an oil and vinegar dressing, French dressing or a dip. They are usually arranged in a decorative pattern on a large flat dish or tray, from which people help themselves. Suitable items to include are:

1) apples (cubed, dipped in lemon juice)
2) black or green olives
3) carrots (cut into matchsticks)
4) cauliflower florets (blanched)
5) celery (raw or blanched, sliced thinly)
6) courgettes (unpeeled, cut into matchsticks)
7) cucumber (cubed or sliced thickly)
8) fennel (raw or blanched, sliced thinly)
9) green or red pepper (cut in rings or strips)
10) radishes (small, whole)
11) spring onions
12) tomatoes (thin wedges, slices, or if small, halved)

SOURED CREAM DIP

3–4 helpings

½ clove of garlic
1 × 15ml spoon/1 tablespoon chilli sauce
1 × 5ml spoon/1 teaspoon creamed horseradish
1 × 15ml spoon/1 tablespoon Worcestershire sauce
½ × 2.5ml spoon/¼ teaspoon dry mustard
a pinch of Cayenne pepper
1 × 5ml spoon/1 teaspoon lemon juice
250ml/½ pint soured cream

Crush the garlic. In a small basin, combine all the ingredients. Chill for 2–3 hours to allow the flavours to develop.
    Serve with crudités.

Crudités and *Soured Cream Dip*

STUFFED TOMATO SALAD

4 helpings

4 large firm tomatoes
salt

lettuce leaves

STUFFING

½ small tomato
3 × 2.5ml spoons/1½ teaspoons
   olive oil
3 × 2.5ml spoons/1½ teaspoons
   chopped onion
3 × 2.5ml spoons/1½ teaspoons
   chopped pimento
½ clove of garlic

3 × 2.5ml spoons/1½ teaspoons
   chopped ham
salt and pepper
2 eggs
2 × 15ml spoons/2 tablespoons
   butter

Cut the tops off the tomatoes, and remove the cores, seeds, and juice with a small spoon, leaving a firm cup of skin and flesh. Keep the tops if desired. (The cores and juice can be sieved for use in a sauce or added to tomato juice.) Sprinkle the tomato cups inside with salt, and turn upside-down on a plate to drain for 30 minutes.

Meanwhile, make the stuffing. Skin, de-seed and chop the tomato. Heat the oil in a saucepan, add the onion and pimento, and simmer, covered, for a few minutes until they soften. Meanwhile, crush the garlic. Add it to the pan with the chopped ham and tomato, and simmer, uncovered, until the liquid has evaporated. Season with salt and pepper and leave to cool. Scramble the eggs in the butter. Leave to cool under buttered paper. When cold, mix with the onion and pimento mixture.

Fill the tomato cups with the stuffing. Remove the stalks from the tops and replace them on the stuffed tomatoes if desired. Serve the tomatoes on a bed of lettuce leaves.

STUFFED AUBERGINES

4 helpings

2 large aubergines
salt
4 × 15ml spoons/4 tablespoons oil

1 × 15ml spoon/1 tablespoon
grated Parmesan cheese

STUFFING

100g/4oz mushrooms
1 medium-sized onion
1 large tomato
50g/2oz soft white breadcrumbs

1 × 15ml spoon/1 tablespoon
chopped parsley
pepper

Cut the aubergines in half lengthways. Score the flesh with a knife, sprinkle with salt and leave for 30 minutes for the excess water to drain off. Rinse and dry thoroughly on soft kitchen paper. Brush the aubergines with a little of the oil and cook under a low grill for about 20 minutes or until tender. Remove the aubergine pulp to within 6mm–1.25cm/¼–½ inch of the skin, and chop this finely. Reserve the skins and pulp.

To make the stuffing, clean the mushrooms, skin the onion, and chop both finely. Heat 2 × 15ml spoons/2 tablespoons of the oil in a small saucepan and fry the mushrooms and onion gently for 5 minutes. Skin and chop the tomato. Add to the mushrooms and onion with most of the breadcrumbs, the parsley, aubergine pulp, and seasoning.

Pile the mixture back into the aubergine cases and place in an ovenproof dish. Mix the remaining breadcrumbs with the cheese. Sprinkle this over the stuffing and moisten with the remaining oil. Bake in a fairly hot oven, 200°C/400°F/Gas 6, for 20 minutes.

AUBERGINE PÂTÉ

1 large aubergine
1 × 2.5 ml spoon/½ teaspoon salt
a pinch of pepper
1 × 15ml spoon/1 tablespoon
   mayonnaise
1 × 5ml spoon/1 teaspoon lemon
   juice

1 × 5ml spoon/1 teaspoon
   concentrated tomato purée
3 × 2.5ml spoons/1½ teaspoons
   chopped chives *or* spring onions

GARNISH

tomato slices
olives

cucumber slices

Wash and dry the aubergine. Pierce it in several places with a fork. Grill until the skin begins to split and the flesh is soft. Peel the flesh and mash it in a bowl with the other ingredients. Chill, well covered, for a few minutes before serving. Serve on lettuce leaves, on small saucers, garnished with tomato slices, olives, and cucumber slices.

Eat with thin crackers or rye bread.

Aubergine Pâté

EGG & CHEESE DISHES

EGG RÉMOULADE

──────── *4 helpings* ────────

4 hard-boiled eggs
4 × 15ml spoons/4 tablespoons
   thick mayonnaise

1 × 2.5ml spoon/½ teaspoon
   anchovy essence

GARNISH

tomato
gherkin

4 crisp lettuce leaves

Cut the eggs in half lengthways. Pat dry with kitchen paper. Mix together the mayonnaise and anchovy essence. Turn the eggs, cut side down and coat the white outside with the mayonnaise mixture. Arrange small pieces of tomato or gherkin on top. Place 2 egg halves, cut side down, on each lettuce leaf.

STUFFED EGGS

4 hard-boiled eggs
25g/1oz softened butter
1 × 15ml spoon/1 tablespoon
  mayonnaise

salt and pepper
½ × 15ml spoon/½ tablespoon
  Worcestershire sauce (optional)

GARNISH

parsley sprigs, tomato,
  sliced gherkin, stuffed olives,
  radishes

Cut the eggs in half lengthways. Remove the yolks carefully and press through a fine sieve into a bowl, or mash with a fork. Trim a small slice off the rounded side of each half white so that they stand firmly. Mix the yolks with the butter, mayonnaise, salt, and pepper. Add Worcestershire sauce, if liked. Beat until smooth and creamy, put into a forcing bag with a 1.25cm/½ inch star nozzle and pipe into the egg whites. Garnish with a small piece of parsley or tomato, a slice of gherkin, stuffed olive or a radish.

Serve on curled lettuce leaves or watercress sprigs.

**EGG-STAND FOR THE BREAKFAST-
TABLE.**

CASED EGGS AND MUSHROOMS

125g/5oz butter	5 eggs
6 medium thick slices white bread	75ml/3 fl oz milk
2 sticks celery *or* 1 onion	salt and pepper
50g/2oz mushrooms	100g/4oz continental sausage

GARNISH

lettuce leaves   watercress sprigs

Melt 100g/4oz of the butter, and let it cool but not solidify. Cut the crusts off the bread. Brush the butter generously on to both sides of each slice so that the bread is saturated, especially at the corners. Press into individual bun tins so that the corners stick upwards, and trim neatly, if necessary. Bake in a fairly hot oven at 200°C/400°F/Gas 6, for 15–20 minutes until golden-brown. Take care that the tips do not brown too much. Leave to cool.

Slice the celery or skin and chop the onion finely. Slice the mushrooms. Melt half the remaining butter in a pan and sauté the celery or onion for 3–4 minutes until softened. Add the mushrooms and cook for 2–3 minutes until tender. Drain.

Beat the eggs, milk, salt, and pepper together lightly. Melt the remaining butter, pour in the beaten egg, reduce the heat and cook gently, stirring all the time, until the mixture is just set and creamy. Cut the sausage into 6mm/¼ inch dice and add to the scrambled egg with the sautéed vegetables. Stir lightly. Leave to cool. Spoon the cold egg into the bread cases.

Serve on lettuce leaves, garnished with small watercress sprigs.

Cased Eggs and Mushrooms

POACHED EGGS BELLE HÉLÈNE

6–8 helpings

50 heads asparagus	salt
500ml/1 pint milk	50g/2oz butter
1 large lettuce	50g/2oz flour
1 medium-sized onion	7–9 eggs
1 bay leaf	pepper
3 sprigs thyme	1 × 5ml spoon/1 teaspoon lemon juice

Scrape the white stalks of the asparagus and cut off the points. Put the milk into a saucepan and bring to the boil. Shred the lettuce finely and skin and chop the onion. Add to the pan with the bay leaf, thyme, and a little salt; then put in the asparagus stalks. Simmer gently for about 15 minutes or until the stalks are tender. Drain the asparagus, and rub through a fine stainless steel or nylon sieve. Melt the butter in a second pan, add the flour and cook for 1 minute. Remove from the heat and stir in the asparagus purée. Return to the heat and bring to the boil, stirring all the time until the sauce thickens. Beat one of the eggs lightly, stir it into the sauce and continue stirring over very gentle heat, without boiling, until the sauce is very thick. Season the sauce well and add the lemon juice. Cook the asparagus points in boiling salted water for 5 minutes or until tender. Drain well. Poach the eggs and trim neatly to a round shape. Chop the trimmings finely and add them to the sauce. Spoon the sauce in a line down the centre of a heated serving dish. Arrange an equal number of eggs on each side and garnish the top of the sauce, between the eggs, with the asparagus points.

Serve as a first course at dinner.

EGGS IN ASPIC

4 helpings

4 eggs   500ml/1 pint liquid aspic jelly

DECORATION

1 *or* 2 of the following: prawns,
    shrimps, chervil, tarragon,
    cress, watercress, cooked
    peas

GARNISH

cress *or* watercress sprigs

Poach the eggs in water until the whites are firm and the yolks semi-set. Drain on soft kitchen paper and leave to cool. Trim the eggs with a pastry cutter or sharp knife so they will fit into dariole moulds. Chill the eggs and 4 moulds in the refrigerator. Put a little of the jelly in each mould. Rotate, tilting the mould so that the inside becomes entirely coated with a thin layer of jelly. Chill until set. Arrange a decoration of prawns, leaves or peas on the set jelly, using a long pin or fine skewer to set them in place. Add another layer of jelly carefully. Return to the refrigerator to set. Place 1 egg in each mould and add enough jelly to cover it. Return the moulds and any remaining jelly to the refrigerator. When the jellied eggs are firmly set, turn them out on to a dish. Chop the remaining jelly and arrange round the eggs. Garnish with cress or watercress sprigs.

Note 1 × 15ml spoon/1 tablespoon Madeira or dry sherry can be added to the aspic jelly for an extra rich flavour.

CHEESE PÂTÉ

125g/5oz Roquefort *or* other blue cheese
125g/5oz full-fat soft cheese
1 × 15ml spoon/1 tablespoon softened butter
125g/5oz Cheddar cheese
75g/3oz walnuts

1 × 2.5ml spoon/½ teaspoon Worcestershire sauce
1 × 2.5ml spoon/½ teaspoon paprika
a pinch of Cayenne pepper
chopped parsley

Crumble the blue cheese. Blend together with the soft cheese and butter with the back of a spoon. Grate the Cheddar cheese finely and work it in. Chop the walnuts finely. Add them to the mixture with the Worcestershire sauce, paprika, and Cayenne pepper and mix well. Shape the cheese mixture into a ball. Roll in enough parsley to cover completely. Cover with clingfilm and chill.

Serve in small wedges on lettuce leaves, with slices of toast or pumpernickel.

Cheese Pâté

ZÉPHIRE OF CHEESE

4–6 helpings

25g/1oz gelatine
4 × 15ml spoons/4 tablespoons
cold water
325ml/13 fl oz milk
50g/2oz Cheddar cheese
125ml/¼ pint double cream

50g/2oz grated Parmesan cheese
salt and pepper
a good pinch of grated nutmeg

GARNISH

chopped aspic jelly
watercress sprigs

strips of pimento

Soften the gelatine in the cold water in a small heatproof container.
Stand the container in a pan of hot water and stir until the gelatine
dissolves. Cool slightly, and mix into the milk. Chill until cold but
not set. Meanwhile, grate the Cheddar cheese and whip the cream
until semi-stiff. Mix both cheeses, the cream, and seasoning to
taste into the cold milk when it is beginning to thicken. Pour the
mixture into wetted individual moulds or one 625ml/1¼ pint
fluted jelly mould. Chill until set, then turn out, and garnish with
the chopped jelly, watercress, and pimento.

CHEESE CREAM

4 helpings

50g/2oz Cheddar *or* Gruyère
   cheese
dry English mustard
a pinch of Cayenne pepper
a pinch of salt

25g/1oz grated Parmesan cheese
4 × 15ml spoons/4 tablespoons
   aspic jelly
125ml/¼ pint double cream

GARNISH

watercress sprigs

Cayenne pepper

Grate the Cheddar or Gruyère cheese very finely. Season it with a little mustard, a pinch of Cayenne pepper, and a good pinch of salt. Mix in the Parmesan cheese. Warm the aspic jelly until just liquid if set; cool it until quite cold but still liquid. Meanwhile, whip the cream until semi-stiff. Stir the liquid aspic jelly into the whipped cream, blending lightly but thoroughly. Fold in the cheeses lightly, a little at a time; do not beat or the mixture will lose its lightness. Turn the mixture into a 375ml/¾ pint glass bowl or individual bowls, and leave to set. When cold, garnish with watercress sprigs which have been dusted lightly with Cayenne pepper.

Overleaf
From the left
Zéphire of Cheese (page 44), *Cheese Ramekins (page 49)* and
Eggs in Aspic (page 41)

CAMEMBERT OR BRIE SOUFFLÉ

100g/4oz ripe Camembert *or* Brie
cheese
100g/4oz cottage *or* curd cheese
1 × 10ml spoon/1 dessertspoon
gelatine

125ml/¼ pint whole *or* skimmed
milk
salt
2 egg whites

Cut the crusts off the Camembert or Brie cheese. Sieve or mash
with the cottage or curd cheese until both are smooth and
well-blended. Soften the gelatine in the milk in a small heatproof
container. Stand in very hot water, and stir until the gelatine
dissolves. Leave to cool, then mix with the cheeses and seasoning.
Chill. Whisk the egg whites until stiff but not dry. When the
cheese mixture is beginning to set at the edges, fold in the egg
whites lightly but thoroughly. turn into a wetted 500ml/1 pint
soufflé dish, and chill until set.

CHEESE RAMEKINS

4 helpings

25g/1oz Cheshire cheese
50ml/2 fl oz milk (approx)
25g/1oz soft white breadcrumbs
(approx)
25g/1oz grated Parmesan cheese

25g/1oz softened unsalted butter
1 egg
salt and pepper
a pinch of ground mace
butter for greasing

Grate the Cheshire cheese finely. Heat the milk and pour just enough over the breadcrumbs to cover them. Leave to stand for 5–10 minutes. Stir in both cheeses and the butter. Separate the egg, and mix the yolk into the cheese mixture. Season well with salt, pepper and mace. Whisk the egg white until very stiff. Stir one spoonful into the cheese mixture, then fold in the rest. Turn the mixture gently into 4 small greased ovenproof pots or ramekins. Bake in a fairly hot oven at 200°C/400°F/Gas 6, for 15–20 minutes, or until risen and slightly browned. Serve as soon as possible before they sink.

MACE.

FISH & SHELLFISH DISHES

SMOKED SALMON

Slice the salmon very thinly and serve with lemon wedges, Cayenne pepper, and brown bread and butter. Alternatively, form thicker slices into cornets and secure with cocktail sticks, if necessary.

TARAMASALATA

4 helpings

100g/4oz smoked cod's roe
1 clove of garlic
2 × 15ml spoons/2 tablespoons
  lemon juice
4 × 15ml spoons/4 tablespoons
  olive oil

2 × 15ml spoons/2 tablespoons
  cold water
freshly ground black pepper

Skin the roe and garlic. Pound them in a mortar with the lemon juice until smooth. Add small amounts of oil and water alternately until the mixture is completely blended. Season to taste with black pepper, and serve with pita bread.

Smoked Salmon

MRS BEETON'S DRESSED WHITEBAIT

―――――――― *3–4 helpings* ――――――――

50g/2oz flour
salt and pepper
100g/4oz whitebait

milk
fat for deep frying
Cayenne pepper

GARNISH
parsley sprigs
lemon wedges

Season the flour with salt and pepper. Wash the whitebait, dip in milk, and coat with flour, by shaking them together in a tea-towel or plastic bag. Make sure that the fish are separate. Heat the fat to 190–195°C/375–383°F, and fry the fish in small batches until crisp. Check that the fat is at the correct temperature before putting in each batch. When all the fish are fried, sprinkle with salt and Cayenne pepper. Serve immediately, garnished with parsley and lemon wedges, with thinly cut brown bread and butter.

Note Whitebait are eaten whole.

HERRING ROLLS

4 helpings

4 salted *or* rollmop herrings
2 hard-boiled eggs
8 anchovy fillets

25g/1 oz butter
Cayenne pepper
lemon juice

GARNISH

8 lemon slices
4–6 sliced gherkins

1 small diced beetroot
chopped parsley

If using salted herrings, soak them in cold water for several hours, then fillet, and remove all the bones. If using rollmop herrings, divide each into 2 fillets. Separate the egg yolks and whites. Chop the anchovy fillets and egg yolks finely, and mix them with the butter and pepper. Spread most of the anchovy mixture on the herring fillets and roll up firmly. Spread the remaining mixture thinly on the round ends of each roll. Chop the egg whites finely and use to coat the spread end of the rolls. Sprinkle the rolls with a little lemon juice and garnish with lemon slices, gherkins, beetroot, and parsley.

THE HERRING.

SPANISH PRAWNS

5–6 helpings

75ml/3 fl oz cooking oil
1 clove of garlic
a small bunch of chives
500g/1lb cooked shell-on prawns

2 × 15ml spoons/2 tablespoons dry
  sherry
salt and black pepper

Pour the oil into a large flat pan, and heat for a few minutes. Crush the garlic, chop the chives, and add to the oil. Put the prawns (with the shells) in the pan with the sherry. Season with salt and black pepper. Cover the pan and cook for 5 minutes, turning the prawns once.

Serve in small bowls, with crusty French bread. Hand paper napkins and fingerbowls separately.

Spanish Prawns

CUCUMBER CASSOLETTES

1 large *or* 2 thin cucumbers
olive oil
vinegar
salt and pepper
200g/7oz crabmeat *or* cooked *or*
  canned red salmon

3 × 15ml spoons/3 tablespoons
  mayonnaise
Tabasco sauce
65g/2½oz canned anchovy fillets

GARNISH

chopped parsley

Peel the cucumbers and cut them into 5cm/2 inch thick pieces. Remove the seeds with an apple corer or potato peeler. Place the rings on a dish and pour a little oil and vinegar over them; season well. Pound the crabmeat or salmon and mix it with the mayonnaise and a few drops of Tabasco sauce. Drain the cucumber pieces and fill the centres with the fish mixture. Drain the anchovy fillets and twist one round the top of each cucumber ring. Garnish with parsley. Serve on small round croûtes or biscuits if desired.

PRAWN COCKTAIL

— 4 helpings —

4 lettuce leaves
200g/7oz peeled prawns
5 × 15ml spoons/5 tablespoons
  mayonnaise
1 × 15ml spoon/1 tablespoon
  concentrated tomato purée *or*
  tomato ketchup

a pinch of Cayenne pepper *or* a few
  drops Tabasco sauce
salt (optional)
1 × 5ml spoon/1 teaspoon vinegar
  or tarragon vinegar (optional)

GARNISH

4 shell-on prawns

Shred the lettuce leaves. Place a little shredded lettuce at the bottom of 4 glass dishes. Put the prawns on top. Mix the mayonnaise with the tomato purée or ketchup and add a pinch of Cayenne pepper or a few drops of Tabasco sauce. Season with salt and vinegar if required. Pour the mayonnaise over the prawns and garnish each dish with an unshelled prawn.

Serve with rolled brown bread and butter.

THE PRAWN.

MEAT DISHES

PROSCIUTTO CON FICHI
(Smoked Ham with Fresh Figs)

---
4 helpings

250g/8oz Parma ham
salad oil
4 large lettuce leaves

250g/8oz fresh figs
8 black olives

The ham should be cut in paper-thin slices. Brush each slice lightly with a little oil and place on the lettuce leaves. Cut a cross in the top of each fig, and open the points out slightly, to imitate the petals of a flower. Arrange the black olives alternately with the figs on the ham.

Prosciutto Con Fichi

HAM RAMEKINS

8 helpings

225g/8oz lean cooked ham
2 eggs
4 × 15ml spoons/4 tablespoons
  milk
½ × 5ml spoon/½ teaspoon dried
  mixed herbs

½ × 2.5ml spoon/¼ teaspoon dry
  mustard
salt and pepper
fat for greasing
paprika

Chop the ham finely. Separate the eggs. Whisk the egg yolks lightly, add the ham, milk, herbs, mustard, salt and pepper, and mix together well. Divide the mixture equally between 8 well-greased ramekin dishes, filling each about three-quarters full. Cook in a fairly hot oven at 190°C/375°F/Gas 5, for 15 minutes until set. Meanwhile, whisk the egg whites until stiff, and add a little salt. Divide the meringue between the dishes, piling it up roughly. Sprinkle with paprika, return the dishes to the oven, and bake them for another 10–15 minutes until crisp and lightly browned. Serve at once.

CHOPPED LIVER

4–5 helpings

1 medium-sized onion
225g/8oz chicken *or* calf's liver
4 × 10ml spoons/4 dessertspoons
  chicken fat

2 hard-boiled eggs
salt and freshly ground pepper

GARNISH

lettuce leaves   tomato slices

Skin and chop the onion. Remove any gristle or tubes from the liver. Heat the chicken fat in a frying pan. Fry the onion with the liver until soft but not brown. Mince the liver, onion, and hard-boiled eggs very finely. Season with salt and freshly ground pepper, and mix to a paste.

Serve on a bed of lettuce leaves, garnished with tomato slices.

ONION.

LIVER PÂTÉ WITH MUSHROOMS

Makes 2.25kg/4½lb (approx)

1kg/2lb lamb's *or* pig's liver
1kg/2lb green bacon, without rinds
1 × 5ml spoon/1 teaspoon salt
freshly ground pepper
a pinch of ground cinnamon *or*
  grated nutmeg

1 small onion
125g/4oz small cup mushrooms
125g/4oz butter *or* margarine
2 eggs
a pinch of dried thyme

GARNISH

3 bay leaves

Remove any skin and tubes from the liver. Chop the bacon. Mince together finely or process in an electric blender. Add the salt, pepper, and cinnamon or nutmeg. Skin the onion and chop it finely; clean and slice the mushrooms. Melt the butter or margarine in a pan and fry the onion and mushrooms gently for 4–5 minutes, turning frequently. Remove from the heat and stir in the liver and bacon. Beat the eggs lightly until liquid and stir them into the mixture.

Put the mixture into a shallow ovenproof casserole or dish with a lid. Sprinkle the surface with thyme and put the bay leaves in a trefoil pattern on top. Cover the dish and stand it in a pan of hot water which comes half-way up the sides. Bake in a cool oven, 150°C/300°F/Gas 2, for 3 hours. When cooked, leave to cool, keeping the lid on the dish. Chill before serving from the dish.